"We have to free half of the human race,
the women,
so that they can help to free
the other half."

— Emmeline Pankhurst

Also by Suzanne Brody

Unearthed (2022, Silver Bow Publishing)

Lunch with Rav Dimi (2021, Silver Bow Publishing)

Mermaid Tears (2019, Silver Bow Publishing)

Dancing in the White Spaces: The Yearly Torah Cycle and More Poems (2007, Wasteland Press)

Etz Chayim She: Modern Poems Grown from Ancient Texts (2015, Wasteland Press)

SERAH'S SECRETS

by

Suzanne Brody

720 Sixth Street, Unit #5
New Westminster, BC
V3L 3C5
CANADA

Title: Serah's Secrets
Author: Suzanne Brody
Publisher: Silver Bow Publishing
Cover Art: "Pastoral Dream" painting by Candice James
Cover Layout and Design: Candice James
Editing: Candice James

All rights reserved including the right to reproduce or translate this book or any portions thereof, in any form without the permission of the publisher. Except for the use of short passages for review purposes, no part of this book may be reproduced, in part or in whole, or transmitted in any form or by any means, either by means electronically or mechanically, including photocopying, recording, or any information or storage retrieval system without prior permission in writing from the publisher or a licence from the Canadian Copyright Collective Agency (Access Copyright).

www.silverbowpublishing.com
info@silverbowpublishing.com
ISBN: 978-1-77403-219-0 paperback
ISBN: 978-1-77403-220-6 electronic book
© Silver Bow Publishing 2022

Library and Archives Canada Cataloguing in Publication

Title: Serah's secrets / by Suzanne Brody.
Names: Brody, Suzanne, 1976- author.
Description: Includes bibliographical references and index.
Identifiers: Canadiana (print) 20220255385 | Canadiana (ebook) 20220255393 | ISBN 9781774032190
  (softcover) | ISBN 9781774032206 (EPUB)
Classification: LCC PS3602.R64 S47 2022 | DDC 813/.6—dc23

Acknowledgements

This book would not have seen the light of day without some very important assistance. Thank you to the ladies of my Women's Torah study group for keeping me on track, believing in me, and sharing my wonder and excitement about this often overlooked person. Thanks also to the students of Kitah Hei at Temple Beth-El in Ithaca for being my first group of readers and for providing their feedback. I cannot say enough about the love, encouragement, enthusiasm, and support of my family in this endeavor. Thank you all.

Serah's Secrets

Introduction

I can't remember when I was first introduced to Serah, but ever since she was pointed out to me, I have been fascinated by her. In a text where men far outnumber the women, her name appears in two lists, set centuries apart, without any other information about who she was or what role she might have played in events. I'm not the first to think she must have led an extraordinary life. In the Medieval time period, multiple Sages recorded tales with Serah as the protagonist. I have done my best to be faithful to as many of these stories as possible while weaving my own narrative, even in cases where contradictory understandings were presented.

Around the time of the Enlightenment, in the 1800s, when rationalist thought was revered above supernatural and mystical explanations of the world, the stories of Serah sank into obscurity. While recent feminist scholarship has revived some interest in this fascinating woman, she is still unknown to the vast majority of people.

The same might also be said of Osnat (whose name also appears as Asnath). 500 years ago, Osnat was a wise scholar at a time when few females received much education. She has been called the world's first female rabbi, though few today know of her and the stories of the miracles she is said to have performed.

Serah's Secrets

Prologue

"Passing the Torch"

It's your turn now
to be the keeper
of time and memory,
to be the rope
holding this people
together,
gently steering them
in the path of God.

My grandmother was right. I knew her right away. I shouldn't sound so surprised, because everything my grandmother ever told me would happen eventually did come to pass. But I had waited so very long for this moment. After centuries of scouring faces, looking into people's souls through their eyes, and traveling from snowy mountaintops to desert dunes at the mere whisper of someone who was capable of just a little bit more than anyone expected, I had started to believe this is the one event my grandmother foretold that would never come to pass. Then, quite by chance, I overheard two women gossiping in the marketplace.

"Did you hear about what happened in Amedi last time the moon was new?"

"No, this is the first time I've been able to get out to market since little Batya was so sick. Even with the priests' visits and the prayers that were said, we feared the worst. At least Yusef was able to bring our vegetables to market and use that sweet face of his to sell them and buy some meat to bring home. With just a sip of soup made from that meat, Batya started to get better, praise the Lord. But, as good as he is at selling, Yusef does not have a good ear for news. I have heard nothing. What happened in Amedi?"

"The synagogue burned!"

"Oh, how awful! What happened? How many were hurt? Do they need our help?

"No one really knows what happened or how the fire started. I've heard either it was an accident when a candle tipped over or it was a wild gang of boys who hate Jews who lit it on fire on purpose. But, however it started, the strange thing is the synagogue burned, but all of the people were out of the building at the time, so no one was hurt."

"How is it that no one was in the building? Weren't there people reciting the prayers over the new moon?"

"For some reason, they were saying their prayers outside. I never did hear why that was. I suppose it's possible someone thought saying the prayer outside felt more authentic because you could actually look up into the sky."

"I'm so glad to hear no one was hurt. But the prayer books? The holy Torah?" The woman sounded either on the verge of hysteria or the verge of tears, It was hard to tell which.

"Completely safe."

"What?!!? How could that be? The building burned but none of the sacred writings? And no one was inside praying as would be expected?"

"And that's not even all!"

"Not all?!?" The astonished woman leaned in closer as her friend lowered her voice.

"They say there was a woman there. A woman who started reciting invocations no one has ever heard before. Heavenly beings appeared in the air, extinguished the fire, then disappeared as mysteriously as they had come."

"Now I know you are making fun of me! Off with you, you evil gossip. I have vegetables to sell."

"Don't be mad at me. You know I am only telling you what I heard. I'm not playing a trick on you!"

I almost walked over to those two women with their heads close together and their gossip like a present between them. I desperately wanted to know the name of this mysterious woman. But I cautioned myself, *'there's no rush'*. I figured I could take the time to walk through the rest of the market and see if others were telling the same story. I didn't want to rush off on the dusty, bumpy journey to Amedi only to find it was just a story meant to get a reaction from a friend.

Over the years, I had encountered far too many situations like that. A whisper of a story or the hint of a woman with magical power or knowledge of the secrets of the universe, and off I would rush. After setting off a few times without even stopping to rent a donkey or fill my water skins, I learned my lesson.

Now before I hurried to find the truth of these rumors, I should at least make sure I was provisioned properly for the journey. It took longer for me to think to verify or corroborate any of these stories. Far too many of them have just been products of fertile imaginations out of the mouths of people who want to be storytellers.

So, with a heart beating faster than a hummingbird's wings, I slowed my steps and strained my ears. I was eager to rush off to find this mysterious woman who could summon heavenly beings and quench fire with the power of her words. It had been decades since I had last heard whispers of stories with even half as much potential.

The world around me was changing like the desert dunes under the influence of the wind, and I was starting to think it was time for me to rest. But not until I had found the one my grandmother had told me about. The one who could take my treasure, protect it, and keep the thread growing.

Then I heard the story again. This time it was no gossiping women with too much interest in other people's business. This time it was the boy with camels to rent talking with someone whose clothes smelled of smoke and whose camel was badly in need of rest and care.

"You and your camel look like you've been through a lot. Where are you coming from, sir?"

"From Amedi. And I would be much obliged if you could spare a bit of water and perhaps a fresh camel."

"Amedi? Where's that?"

"We're ruled by the Kurds, and until recently we lived there in peace. Now I am headed south to deliver news."

"You can share your news with me, sir, before you continue on your journey. In return for your tale, here's the water you asked for and a place in the shade to sit while you drink it."

And for the second time that day, I heard the tale of the synagogue that burned, and the fire that was put out by heavenly beings summoned by an incantation no one had ever heard before. It wasn't a phrase from the prayers. If it was, someone would have been sure to recognize that. And it didn't sound like anything the rabbi remembered learning from his teacher. Besides, the rhythm was all wrong for the types of texts the rabbi knew. The more I heard, the more convinced I became that this woman must have had some training in the mystic tradition.

I could have left right then to gather provisions for a journey to Amedi but decided to wait to possibly garner more information before leaving. Surely we weren't too far away if it was in a place ruled by Kurds. But I still didn't know the name of this powerful woman. Chances were that once I arrived at Amedi, any of the local residents could point her out to me. Unless, of course, she wasn't actually from Amedi but had been drawn there just so she could help save the Jews and the sacred writings. I figured it was probably better if I could learn her name before I left. It would probably make finding her much easier and timely.

So, I sat on a nice flat rock I had found. I closed my ears to the sounds of the market all around me. I stopped hearing the calls of "Carrots! Just picked! Only 2 silver dinars!," "Best camels! Rent by the day or week!" and other such cries. I closed my eyes to the swirl of people and livestock. I focused on my breath slowing down and going in and out. I let the magic word hum along my tongue, drift out with one breath, and in through the nose and the ears on the second and third breaths. For good measure, I released the magic word a second time.

Then, ever so faintly, I felt a tickle on my ear. I heard the wind whisper a single word: *'Osnat'*. It sounded like the mixture of a sigh and a prayer. *'Osnat'*.

Having fooled myself into believing I heard other names previous times I tried this simple spell. I cautioned myself not to get my hopes up too much. Still, it was enough to add a little extra speed to my step as I began to gather all I might need for my journey.

Chapter 1: The Beginning

"The Melody of Power"

Words tickle my tongue
like butterflies
dancing from my body
and coloring the air.
Songs pour forth,
bubbling brooks
winding through my days
and I create the world around me,
unaware
of my own power.

As the donkey brought me closer and closer to Amedi, I started to hear the wind singing in my grandmother's voice, repeating her words from so long ago. *"You will know when it's time to give the secret and the blessing to another. After you train her and she is ready, the chariot will come to take you to heaven."* Only this time, I also heard another word, one that I'm sure I never heard my grandmother say,. 'Osnat'.

I arrived in Amedi a bit dusty but cautiously optimistic. The closer I got to the town, the more I heard things about this unusual woman. In the Camel's Inn, I overheard a group of young men talking in between slurps of soup. They seemed to be trying to figure out to whom a dove found on the ground belonged. I got the impression these fine young fellows were honest men who really cared about returning this lost dove to the rightful owner. But they weren't sure whether it rightfully belonged to Mr. Feathers who owned three separate dovecotes, or to Mr. Proxim whose small dovecote might have been slightly closer to the actual place where the dove had been found.

I wasn't particularly interested in who owned this particular dove, but it was impossible to ignore their conversation. Their voices rose as each of the young men tried to convince the other that he knew the right answer and the proper thing to do. Their strident voices were so loud, that all other conversations around the room stopped. Some of the diners looked like they were trying to ignore the vehement young men. Others tried to slink out, taking a path designed to keep them as far away as possible from the fists pounding the table to mark emphasis. I considered doing the same, but stayed rooted to my seat, hostage to a rumbling belly. And, I will admit, the longer I sat there, the more I came under the influence of some curiosity about how this argument would play out.

Having seen similar scenes in other Inns during my travels, I amused myself by trying to guess which of the two most common outcomes to such scenes would play out this time. I was caught slightly off guard when I noticed one of the other lodgers at the Inn stand up and approach the conversation with languid, unhurried steps. This was not part of the usual sequence of events as far as these sort of things go. My gaze scanned his face, and rather than the expected anger or anticipation, I noticed an almost unnatural calm cross his eyes and mouth. He spoke with a soft voice, and I will admit to leaning a bit closer to hear what he was going to say to the excited youths.

After asking if these young gentlemen truly did not know the answer to the question based on their studies of the sacred texts, rather than jumping into the argument with his own logic or prooftexts, he gave them some advice. I was not entirely surprised to hear the lodger recommend that the young men consult a rabbi, a teacher, who could teach them how such disputes are resolved. What did make my heart leap a little and put a hint of a smile on my face, was hearing that one particular, extraordinarily wise and well-learned teacher and Head of a Yeshiva was being recommended as the best person to educate these young men: Osnat. In Amedi.

"I must be on the right path," I thought to myself. With as many signs as this, I wouldn't even need to pull on my song magic to extract information from people I might encounter on the road. I've learned that song magic can be used for a great number of things, but using magic takes a lot of concentration and energy, so sometimes it really is easier to do things the "normal" way rather than call on the magic that comes from bringing words and melodies together. Besides, I like to think of myself as a good person, and good people don't just go around manipulating others for their own needs or pleasure.

Sometimes, though, it seems that the only way to move forward on a quest or keep other people safe is to extract information from a person when they otherwise wouldn't have been too happy sharing it freely. Fortunately, that didn't seem to be the case this time, and my conscience could rest easy. All I had to do was pay attention to what I was seeing and hearing around me, and I would finally find what I was looking for, someone to take my gift and become the next living memory of our people.

The journey must have tired me out more than I had thought, because those were the last thoughts I remember before lifting my face off the table and discovering the pattern of the table's grooves etched into my cheek. It was not like me to just nod off like that. I wondered whether my age was starting to catch up to me the closer I came to finding Osnat. Such a phenomenon would not be beyond the realm of possibility, but maybe the simpler explanation was just that it had been a long day and concentrating so hard on everything around one can be pretty draining. Plus, both the atmosphere and the food here were very calming. Having found a way to at least pretend to justify my unusual nap to myself while avoiding too much self-recrimination, I sat up a bit straighter and looked around.

The youths who had been arguing about the ownership of the dove were no longer anywhere in the room. In fact, the room itself was quite a bit darker than when I had first sat down, and there were far fewer people overall. I looked for the innkeeper and asked for a room for the night. Luckily, the Inn was not full and I was soon asleep and dreaming of songs floating over meadows, deserts, and towns. The songs curled themselves into the shapes of the ancient letters of our people and started moving themselves around as if they were trying to form a word or a thought. But, before their meaning could become clear, the sun landed on my eyelids, and the world of dreams disappeared as I sat up and rubbed my eyes.

Before my feet touched the floor, my thoughts sorted themselves out. I remembered where I was, why I was here, and what I needed to do. It was unfortunate I had fallen asleep at the table last night before learning where those young gentlemen were headed. I figured, there couldn't be all that many schools run by women around the area. It should be a simple thing to ask directions.

But what would people think of a woman like me asking for the yeshiva? Being no stranger to danger, I thought it best to conceal the true nature of my quest and instead assume a different persona. I asked myself what type of woman might be looking for a particular yeshiva. A wife? A mother? A sister? A matchmaker? I looked at myself in the basin of water that had been left in my room so I could wash my hands and face.

While I certainly did not look hundreds of years old, I also did not appear to be young enough to be one of the student's sisters. Nor, I realized, would a young sister have been likely to undertake a journey of such length to find her sibling, especially unaccompanied. A son might be expected to resemble his mother, and a groom would hopefully recognize whether someone was actually his bride or not. So in the end, I decided that pretending to be a matchmaker was the best way to be able to move around town asking of the whereabouts of the yeshiva and its leader without arousing suspicion. That settled in my mind, I gathered my belongings, and headed downstairs for breakfast and to settle my bill with the innkeeper.

With a full belly and a much-diminished purse, I retrieved my donkey from the stable and set out in what I hoped was the right direction to the main market of Amedi. The market, I have found, is usually the best place to pick up information of almost any sort. The market of Amedi, while small and lacking a certain diversity of wares, did not disappoint when it came to what I was hoping to find.

Before nightfall, I had heard the story of the miraculous saving of lives and scrolls at the synagogue multiple times, and many other rumors about miracles Osnat had performed as well. Perhaps even more importantly, at the market, I learned where I could find Osnat. But, as the sky grew dark and the marketplace emptied, I realized I had spent the day gathering information and had not stopped to make arrangements for the night. I'm no stranger to sleeping under the stars, and while that's a perfectly acceptable way to spend the night out in the fields, country, or desert, it was not looked upon favorably in the cities and towns. Fortunately, one of the women with whom I had spoken earlier was still there, closing down her market stall. Remembering that she had mentioned a daughter of marriageable age who might make a beautiful bride for a young yeshiva student, I decided to see if I could prevail upon her hospitality for the night. At first, the woman was reluctant to invite me to her home.

"Our daughter is beautiful and kind and knows how to keep a clean home and mend clothing, but we ourselves are not so rich, you understand. We don't have an extra room or a bed stuffed with feathers. Surely our home is too humble for a matchmaker such as yourself."

I could see merely stating that I didn't need much or trying to convince this woman with either humbleness or fancy arguments was not going to get me a place where I could sleep that night with a roof over my head. But, by now, the market was practically deserted. I could see dancing candlelight and peaceful family scenes through some nearby windows, but the very solid doors did not give me hope that they would open up to a stranger's knock. So, as the woman turned to walk toward home, softly, I began to hum under my breath. Into the hum, I breathed suggestions of the great value of hospitality and the rewards of doing good deeds. My tongue still vibrating with the end of the incantation, the woman turned around.

"Humble as our home is, we are still always able to find another chair for someone like yourself to join us for the evening meal.... And we do have straw to sleep upon..." As her hesitant voice trailed off, I gratefully accepted her offer of hospitality for the night. In the morning, I would find my way to the yeshiva and to Osnat.

***

Standing outside of the door marked "Rosh Yeshiva," I suddenly realized that having made it this far, for one of the few times in my life, I was at a loss for words. How do you tell someone you've never met that you have come to make them your successor? How do you expose them to their destiny without them wondering about your sanity? It seems to me it's so much harder to do all of that when the person whose life you are about to change is already an adult.

    I took a calming breath and knocked. A melodic voice welcomed me in and offered me a seat. Before I sat down, I checked to be sure the woman before me was, in fact, Osnat.

    Satisfied I had found the person I was looking for, the next thing I had to do was find out if the stories I had been hearing along my journey were true. Putting a bit of awe and wonder into my voice, I wove a spell for truth into my questions about what I had heard about this woman.

    Without hesitation, in a lyrical voice, Osnat confirmed the stories I heard really did happen. A sigh of relief rose up into my throat, as Osnat's assistant poked her head into the room. Apologizing for disturbing us, she let Osnat know that a woman had just brought in a very sick child.

    With a nod, I assented to the question in Osnat's eyes and the woman and child were brought into the room where we were sitting. I cannot tell you how she did it, but I can say that I witnessed with my own eyes the fact that Osnat was able to provide a cure. As she sent the grateful woman and child on their way, Osnat told me she often dreamed of her deceased father, and last night he came to her and told her how to cure this child. Before she had even gotten around to asking my name, she shared some of her poetry with me, and we had a nice conversation about literature. As pleasant as our conversation was, we both knew I had not come all this way just to share a love of words with another remarkable woman. I knew it was finally time for me to tell someone my story.

    Osnat sat calmly and serenely awaiting my words.

Chapter 2 – Serah's Childhood

"Origins"

I was wrapped in love
overpowering the losses,
learned a definition
of family
without biological entanglements,
cradled
in the gentle breeze
of song
tickling my ear.

I was sure that Osnat must be a busy woman. On my way to her office, I had heard the hum of a multitude of voices all striving to find Truth and Wisdom. I had picked out the cadence and notes of a song that stretched back to the beginning of binding together a people. At the time, I hadn't paid much attention, as I was intent on my own quest.

Before I could open up to her and share the gift (and its burden) with this pale young woman in front of me, I needed to know if she truly was the one I had been looking for. Many years ago, I had made the mistake of confiding in someone based on the whispers I'd followed from the marketplace. The signs I'd seen and heard were not so different from the ones that brought me to be sitting in this cozy room across from this woman with wise brown eyes.

With a soft intake of air, I breathed in the strength of the black letters and the mysteries of the white spaces between them. I tasted the dusty past and felt a cool spring begin to unwind my tongue. A gentle spell wrapped around us, and even if a dozen students had burst into the room, neither of us would have noticed them, and they would have all left with no understanding or recollection of anything we said.

I could have reached inside her heart and head, pulling out her life's story and finding answers to all my questions, but that wasn't how I like to treat other people. Especially if Osnat was the one who would carry on after me, she deserved to be treated with courtesy and respect. As the head of a school, I'm sure Osnat was used to questions, which may explain how her face reflected a neutral, yet friendly and curious demeanor even as my questions became more unusual. Finally satisfied, I felt my heart sing in harmony with breaths I didn't know I had been holding, and my whole body relaxed.

In the momentary lull between the last of my questions and the first of Osnat's, the air shimmered with the magic of those voices from the other room, and I caught glimpses of letters trailing flames and sprouting wings. Clearly, there was some strong magic being practiced here. I could only hope I was correct and Osnat herself was, indeed, the source of this magic. Her voice rang with the sound of butterflies dancing from flower to flower. It was clear I had aroused her curiosity, and she leaned toward me in anticipation. As much as I wanted to jump right in with the reason I specifically sought her out, I had the feeling to do so would scare her away, and I might then be forced to wait hundreds of years before the next opportunity presented itself.

Having seen for myself the importance of courtesy, choice of words, and tone of voice, I began my own story by first thanking Osnat for answering my questions. I explained I had asked all my questions because I was looking for someone in particular, someone like me with magic singing in her soul and shaping the world around her. I then begged her indulgence for a bit more of her time so that I might introduce myself properly.

I began with the most basic of introductions. My name is Serah bat Asher, and there is a lot about my life that is not quite what it seems. I began weaving a low hum around my words. Though it sounds like a tale told around the fire when the current wine is plentiful, I assure you that each word I speak to you is spun of the purest truth.

For as long as I can remember, I have been known as Serah bat Asher, Serah the daughter of Asher. To say that my father was Asher, however, is not, in fact, the whole truth. It is true that I was raised in the household of a man named Asher, and he did treat me like a member of the family. It's even possible he treated me the same way he would have treated his own biological daughter if he'd had one. But all of Asher's other children, the ones who actually shared his blood, were boys, and they were younger than I was.

When I was a child, it was really the women who spent time with me and cared for me, making me feel safe, secure, and loved. I didn't realize it at the time, but I had a most unusual childhood. from listening to the older women's chatter as they shelled peas and kneaded bread, I knew from an early age that in the time before my own memories were formed, I had a different father. He was not Asher, but I don't know who he was. I never once heard anyone slip and use his name, and the closest I came to knowing anything about him was when my grandmother told me I was just like him. As I grew older, I learned the main reason my first father's name was never mentioned. Names have power, especially after death and in families like ours where magic sings in the blood. Calling on a dead person by name can bring forth ghosts, and not all ghosts are pleasant or beneficial.

My mother's name was Hadurah; a name that perfectly describes her. Hadurah means elegant, refined, impressive, and to me, my mother was the most elegant and impressive of all of the women in our extended family. We weren't exactly a poor family. We had herds of sheep and cattle, at least when I was young, and my mother brought rare and beautiful fabrics with her as part of her dowry when she married Asher. Even after years of wear and washing, when the fabric had grown thinner and sprouted snakes of stitches holding together rips and holes, my mother still managed to make those dresses look like the most elegant and refined dresses found anywhere in the whole world.

She wasn't the sort of person who yells or hits to get her way. Her voice had a soft, commanding tone that somehow demanded obedience and made you happy to acquiesce. I used to think that was just because my mother was the best ever. Now I wonder if there wasn't a bit of magic in her words and the tone in which she said them.

Given my own gifts, it would certainly make sense. They do say magic runs in families. I wonder if she would have told me about her own magic if she had lived to see me through my first moon blood. She certainly didn't say anything when I was a child first struggling to understand and control my gift. By the tightness that crept in around her mouth and the way in which she always seemed to bundle me away when a magic song started to bubble forth, you might even get the impression that she was ashamed of me and my gift. So, my earliest memories are a mixture of wonder and shame.

I remember playing in the mud, joyfully repeating the word over and over and flinging fistfuls of mud into the air, where it turned into birds and butterflies. I wanted to keep playing and watching the mud fly away. But when someone grabbed my wrist to stop me from flinging the next handful of mud into the air, my happy chant turned into a wail. Suddenly, instead of being surrounded by cheerful birds and butterflies, the air became thick with brown bees and angry spiders and I was being told I mustn't ever do that again, even though I had no idea what I had done.

I don't remember ever playing in mud again. But that didn't stop my voice from bringing forth the magic. What began as one-word cries or exclamations of discovery quickly turned into phrases and sentences as my command over language grew along with my mind and body. By the time I was two and a half, and narrating everything I was doing or seeing, it was clear to my mother that very soon she would not be able to either suppress or control my magic on her own. I suppose I must have been a bit of a handful, but that did not deter my mother from also beginning to see suitors.

Asher was kind to me from the beginning. Like my mother, Asher had also buried a spouse. I wanted to sing and dance at their wedding, but I was told that it was too late for me, and I was put to bed. I think my mother was afraid of what might happen if I were allowed to be at the party and sing. Asher didn't know about my gift, and it seemed like my mother wanted to keep it that way, which wasn't hard since I spent my time mostly with the women, and not with my new father and the many other men and boys I met.

I was three years old when Asher brought us to the land of Canaan, to his father Jacob's family estate. Suddenly, I had more uncles and cousins than I ever could have imagined. Our family alone could almost fill an entire town. Sometimes, it was all so overwhelming that I clung to my mother's skirts and buried my eyes and ears in the folds of the fabric. Over time, I came to distinguish faces and personalities from the blur of people and activity around me. I started to hum under my breath again. I whispered songs of joy, love, and sweetness when I spotted the plump aunt who snuck me sweets when I walked by. My words mixed with the sound of tears and pain when I spotted the uncle who always found fault in what my mother and I did.

None of the grownups seemed to pay any attention or notice me humming and singing. But not much escapes the eyes of children. I overheard my cousins one day when we were all out looking for hawthorn berries. Ariel (my uncle Gad's son) and Usi (my uncle Dan's son) had used their long legs to climb just a little bit faster and higher than me. But I was the one who actually found a shadowy gully with the Sinai Hawthorn bushes in it. The lure of the bright red berries drew me from bush to bush as my collection pouch filled one handful at a time. I was deep in the shadows when I heard Ariel and Usi saunter into the gully.

"You really think she's making things happen when she sings those silly little songs?" asked a reedy voice I knew belonged to Usi, the younger of these two cousins.

"How else can you explain it?" asked Ariel. "My mom was super upset about something. Then she walked by, sang something about troubles flying away like crows and turning into doves. Next thing I know, my mom's acting like there was never anything wrong."

"That's just grown-ups for you. Your mom probably saw you there and *'put on a happy face.'* You know your mom almost never lets you see her upset."

"But then what about the time Sunis fell into that cactus? He was yowling louder than a jackal before and after they started pulling those spikes out of his back. The aunts were only halfway done and the noise was shaking the tent. That comely little weirdo walks by stares at Sunis, does that singing under her breath that she does, and walks away. The yowling stops, and Sunis is perfectly calm while the aunts pull out the rest of the cactus spikes."

That's when I realized that my cousins were talking about me. They had noticed the humming and singing I did. I know my mom said I was only supposed to sing in secret. I had gotten in trouble for singing before, in our old home before my mother brought us here. No one else was supposed to know that sometimes my words and tunes had the power to make things happen. I could change people's moods, and make them feel better, but I could also make other things happen with animals sometimes.

Before I learned to control my powers, whenever my mother noticed the magic starting to spill out of me and take effect on the people, animals, or objects around me, she would use one arm to drag me along, and the other to cover up my mouth. But singing these songs was as much a part of me as breathing. So I didn't stop. I was just quieter when I sang or hummed. And I tried to hide from the rest of my new, big family even as I wondered why when I was sad, one of the grandmothers or aunts could wrap me up in a big hug and wipe away my tears while talking softly to me to make me feel better but I couldn't sing my special songs for people. Why was what the older women did ok but what I could do not ok?

I'm so much older now than I was then, and it's still a mystery to me why some people are scared of my songs and others come to me asking me to help them.

Chapter 3 - Grandmother's Wisdom

"Masked Powers"

The stories hide
behind the wrinkles,
and you'd never know
the amazing feats
once performed
by those shaking hands.
She has not
just witnessed history
but shaped it
bent it
to her own moral compass
and added
her own personal touch.
With each grey hair
she grew in power
ready
to join the other titans.

When I was still little enough to be sitting on her knee with my head pillowed by her chest and my body secured by one strong arm, but old enough for my feet to reach halfway down her legs, my grandma started whispering in my ear just before I fell asleep each night. She whispered stories of letters flying to the heavens, of hearts carried on a flying carpet of music, and of the way the entire world was created through the breath of words. Sometimes she would even hum or sing a little for me. When my grandmother sang to me, I saw the whole history of the world unfolding. I watched Adam name the animals, and could hear Noah singing those same animals onto his ark. The sounds of the tower of Babel falling always hurt my ears and made me curl up into a ball in pain. Through my grandmother's notes, I could hear Sarah humming to baby Isaac, and my grandmother calling my own mother forth from her womb.

Then, when my mom's belly was big with one of my half-brothers, my grandmother started taking me on long walks away from all of the others. No one seemed to mind these little oases of time my grandmother created for the two of us. They understood that as much as we loved all of the aunts, uncles, and cousins, and even each of my four half-brothers, we had a special blood bond. I'm guessing that this blood bond is what helped her to recognize my magic early on. But maybe it was just the fact that she and my mother were the only ones there who had seen the effects of my songs before I learned how to control them.

When I was just a baby, first starting to string sounds together, I drew the water up from the well, making it bubble over the top when I clapped and burbled that near-ubiquitous baby sound "babababa." Around the same time, I called a sheep over to me so we could curl up and fall asleep together with a tired "maaaah maaah." The first time these things happened, people thought they were just cute, serendipitous moments. Only my mother and grandmother, the two women who spent the most time caring for me, realized these were not just rare, odd events, but ones I was making happen over and over as I experimented with my voice and its power on the world around me.

By the time my grandmother began formally teaching me on our special walks, I had already figured out a few things about my magic on my own. I knew it seemed to work just as well when I sang softly as it did when I sang loudly, as long as I was putting the same amount of my soul into my words. But it was my grandmother who taught me the importance of choosing the right words at the right time. She taught me that if I was singing to help someone in pain, that person had to have an open heart for the magic to work. It isn't that the person has to fully believe in magic or God or anything in particular. They just have to be open to the possibility of there being wonder, magic, and miracles in this world for my songs to have the intended effect. If the person's heart isn't open even just a tiny crack, my magic could wind up bouncing around having all sorts of unintended consequences. She also cautioned me if I chose the wrong words or intonation, my songs had the power to hurt and cause damage. She made me do things in two ways; the way they should be done and the way deliberately designed to go awry. Practicing those lessons always left me with my heart in tatters, and I had to take time to compose my outward appearance before returning to camp.

I had heard my grandmother tell a lot of stories over the years. She told stories of our ancestors so vividly that I thought I was going to get hit by pieces of the idols that Abraham smashed. In her stories, the power of God was palpable. She shared tales of a bird so big its feet stood on earth while its head reached up to heaven. But even around the fire when both the men and the women were bragging of their exploits and talents, my grandmother did not talk about herself.

One day, as we gathered sticky-sweet dates, my grandmother began to tell me a story of when she was a little girl. So, I froze in astonishment. Then I set down my basket to pay attention. I knew, that unlike the other stories my grandmother told, I might never hear this particular tale ever again.

Like me, my grandmother began to sing magic songs at a young age. That part didn't surprise me. I already knew this particular magic could be passed down by blood, and it most often passed from grandmother to granddaughter. Plus, it was my grandmother who took me on these special walks to teach me. It stood to reason that she was able to teach me because she could do it, too. She was a lot better at hiding it than I was, though. And the story that she told me that day is probably a good part of the reason why.

My grandmother grew up as part of a tribe of nomadic traders. In the rainy months, they would spend time with the craftsmen, regaling their hosts with stories of their travels and exchanging sweet, dried fruits and spices for bowls, clothing, and sometimes even jewelry. In the dry months, they would gather and dry fruit and spices, and in exchange for animals from a flock or something to ease the thirst, the bowls, clothing, and jewelry would be passed along.

One day, my grandmother and her tribe arrived at a village they had never stopped at before. While they were there, my grandmother witnessed a village boy being cruel and attacking one of the younger children of the tribe. My grandmother's anger flared brighter and stronger than it ever had before. Rushing over to help the child, the loud, angry words she didn't even realize she was hurling toward the boy flew ahead of my grandmother. Later, the couple who found the boy crumpled on the ground said it looked as if he had been crushed by a pile of rocks. But no one ever found any rocks anywhere near there. And the villagers there never saw my grandmother's tribe ever again.

Once they had put some distance between themselves and that village, my grandmother's grandmother pulled her aside and gave her the biggest scolding she ever got in her life. My grandmother had already realized what happened to the boy attacking the younger child was all her fault. Her angry words had not just killed someone, but had done so by slamming into him over and over. Not only that, but her own parents, grandmother, and the rest of the tribe were forced to lie and flee in order to keep her safe. After that, my grandmother didn't speak or even hum for many years.

As an adult, I realized my grandmother took that chain of events not just as a lesson to be careful of what and how you say things, but also as a sign that our magic had to be kept secret. She thought if anyone from that town had found out she had killed that boy by using magic, it would be even worse than just finding out she had killed him at all.

But those weren't the lessons I took from my grandmother's story. I thought the moral of the story was not to curse someone or use this magic power of words in anger because of all the bad things that could happen. Besides, when I was a child, I was not good at keeping secrets at all. Maybe there were just too many people around, or we were too much in each other's business. But, when I was young, there were a lot of people in the family camp who knew there was something different, something special, about my singing.

As much as my grandmother tried to downplay my gift, people knew that everyone seemed calmer and happier after I sang to or for them.

Chapter 4 – News

"News"

It comes
dancing in my ear,
playing
with the corners of my mouth
raising my feet
and spinning me around
then slips between my lips
to find
another friendly ear.

My father and his brothers had been gone for a long time. They had gone away like this before when our bellies were crying out with hunger. When they came back, they each carried huge sacks of grain. It looked like so much food I thought we would never run out again. But, the crops still weren't growing, and even I noticed how the piles of grain kept shrinking. We were trying to make the food last as long as we could while we waited for the men to return. Even though they tried to keep their fears away from the children, we could all feel the tension and hear the whispers as my mother and her sisters-in-law worried about bandits or wild animals or the rulers in Egypt. Finally, after days upon days spent waiting, one of the boys spotted the cloud of dust heading toward our tents.

But when they reached us, my father and uncles surprised me. They didn't go straight to grandpa's tent to show him what they brought back. Instead, they huddled around one another, and I caught snatches of their conversation. "If I tell him, he won't believe me!" "Alive is incredible enough, but a ruler, too!" "He'll be so shocked he'll have a heart attack or a stroke!" "We can't not tell him!" "What if we do and he dies? I won't have that on my conscience!"

I don't think they saw me there. I think one of them just suddenly remembered about my special talent. (I told you I wasn't good at keeping it a secret!) They started looking around for me, and found me pretty quickly. That's when they explained what they wanted me to do and why. My uncle Joseph was alive! The uncle who I only knew about from stories and from Grandfather Jacob's weeping. And, he had somehow become the ruler over Egypt! He was the one who was selling us all of this food. When my father and his brothers asked me to tell Grandfather Jacob that Joseph is alive, and he is in Egypt, I knew I had to be careful about how I did this.

I was a fairly skilled player on the harp. So my uncles handed me a harp saying "please, go sit next to our father and strike this harp and speak these words to him. And they instructed me about what I had to say. Then I hurried over to Grandfather Jacob and sat down before him. I let my magic flow as I sang and played the harp. I was told my voice sounded extra sweet as I sang "Joseph my uncle is alive and he rules over all the land of Egypt; he is not dead". For good measure, I made sure to repeat this line over and over so it could gently sink into my grandfather's head and heart. After hearing me sing these words at least two or three times, Grandfather Jacob heard my words and I saw wonder and a smile appear on his face. It was clear to everyone that Jacob was possessed by joy, and through my song the spirit of God had come over him, and he knew all my words were true.

My grandfather blessed me for singing these words before him. At least, I believe he thought he was blessing me. His face would not have looked so radiant if he had intended what came next as a curse. Now, though, looking back over the life I have lived, it feels like it has been both a blessing and a curse. My grandfather looked me in the eyes, cupping my head in his hands, and he said "My daughter, may death never prevail against you, for you have lifted my spirit, and brought me back to life today." Then he asked me to repeat my song once more because it made him so happy. So I sang once more the same words and Jacob listened. I could tell he was pleased.

While my grandfather was still talking with me, my uncles came running over with horses and chariots and royal garments and servants. My grandfather got up and went to meet them. We saw my father and uncles were dressed in royal garments, and they had all the good things Joseph sent with them. That's when my uncles repeated the same news I had just delivered.

"Our brother Joseph is alive, and he rules over the whole land of Egypt".

Even though I'd just said almost the exact same thing, when my grandfather heard my uncles say it, his heart fainted, and he didn't really believe them until he saw all that Joseph had sent along with them. It was a very large amount of food and gifts. Though I think the part that really swayed my grandfather was when my uncles repeated all the signs Joseph had given them.

As they unpacked all the things and displayed all Joseph had sent, my uncles distributed the riches to all of us. Eventually, my grandfather Jacob knew that my father and his brothers had spoken the truth. Slowly, he rose from his seat and said "It is enough that Joseph, my son, is still alive. I will go and see him before I die. I will go down into Egypt, to see my son and my grandchildren." As with everything he did, when my grandfather decided something, it happened.

My grandfather rose up and he put on the garments which Joseph had sent him. They fit him perfectly, and he no longer looked like an old, worn-out man. His back was straighter than I had ever seen it, and to me, he looked like he had grown to twice his size. He washed his face and trimmed and combed his beard. It was the first time I had seen him without a long, tangled beard speckled with pieces of food and sand. Joseph had sent a turban along with the fine, colorful clothes, and my grandfather completed his transformation when he put it on his head. Seeing all of this, all of the grownups ran around with colorful cloth streaming behind them as they rounded up all of us children and herded us into our tents. We all dressed in the new clothes and jewelry that Joseph had sent.

That night, we had a huge party. We were all so excited to know that Joseph was still alive and that he was the ruler over Egypt. Even those of us who had never met Joseph had grown up hearing stories of him, and we were in awe of the idea we had a relative who was that important. The news was so big that all the inhabitants of Canaan heard about it, and they came and rejoiced with us. In fact, we were all so happy and excited that the feast my grandfather prepared lasted for three whole days. It was as if everyone forgot there was still famine in the land and we all filled our mouths and bellies to bursting. All the kings of Canaan, and all the great men of the land ate and drank and made merry in our camp.

Chapter 5 - The Big Move

"Moving"

Lift your feet
so you don't
drag the border line
as foreign
becomes home.
Hug the familiar
to your chest
and open your arms
to embrace the new.
Sometimes
we recognize
the importance of a moment
in the middle of a step.

After the three days of partying, we all got busy packing. One of my cousins who was learning how to be a scribe decided that such a big move was important enough that someone should make a record of it. While the rest of us, no matter how old we were, patched up wagons and baskets and jars or ran around camp gathering the items to fill these containers, my cousin gathered soot from the cooking fires and pounded on gall nuts.

In those days, I couldn't yet read. It wasn't until much later in my life that someone sat by my side and taught me about the magic of the letters. Sometimes I can glimpse it, but the magic of letters was not in my blood the way the magic of song was.

Osnat, who had been sitting silently as I spun the story of my life before her eyes, perked up a bit as I said this. The corners of her mouth twitched toward a smile. It was as if I had suddenly discovered a key to open a door I didn't realize had been locked.

"I have always loved the shapes of the Hebrew letters," Osnat said with a dreamy smile. "I tried not to have favorites, because each was so wonderful by itself. One looked like a mysterious animal, and another, like a creeping vine. Each letter with its own special lines and curves lit up my imagination and danced around my head."

I could tell from those words that Osnat understood how important it was that my cousin wrote all our names down on his parchment.

Jacob brought with him to Egypt his sons and grandsons, his daughters and granddaughters — all his offspring, and my cousin formed the letters for each of our names, grouping us all by our fathers. Maybe that's why my mother and aunts and grandmother weren't recorded along with the rest. Even though there were many others who were a part of our large camp of many tents, my cousin only recorded those of us who were of Jacob's seed. And also me, even though I was not actually born of Jacob's seed but was treated almost my whole life as if I had been. Plus, it may be immodest of me to bring it up, but I was the one my grandfather doted on and referred to as his little songbird when he was feeling particularly sentimental.

Later, during the time we lived in Egypt, one of the scribes showed me where my name was on my cousin's parchment. As he read, he used a thin reed to point to "Asher's sons: Imnah, Ishvah, Ishvi, and Beriah, and their sister Serah." Sometimes, as I was growing up, I wondered whether I truly belonged to this family. I knew my mother had been married before and her first husband was the source of the seed from which I was conceived, but Asher was the only father I ever remembered. So, it felt nice to see other people in my family felt the same way.

I hoped Osnat didn't mind that I skipped pretty far ahead to tell her the next part. But I figured it would be okay because even though it didn't happen until many, many years after our move to Egypt, that's what it's about. Maybe I should explain.

When I was much, much older, and had left Egypt long behind me, I saw some boys I didn't know holding something that looked familiar. I got close enough to be able to hear their conversation. I wasn't trying to spy on them or anything. But I was curious what they were doing with that particular parchment. Plus, they were raising their voices a bit, so it was easy to hear them.

"Daughters? The only daughter Jacob had was Dinah! Even I know the difference between one and many!"

"Maybe there were more who were adopted. Ever think of that? We talk about Michal's children, but her sister Merav is the one who actually gave birth to them. Still, we call them Michal's children because she's the one who did all the work of raising them."

"Okay. That does make some sense. But what about granddaughters? Wasn't Serah Jacob's only granddaughter?"

"Are you forgetting Yocheved?"

"Yocheved? What does Moses' mother have to do with it? She wasn't Jacob's granddaughter! Her husband Amram was Jacob's grandson, but she isn't blood, she married into the family. Besides, you told me 70 people went down to Egypt together."

"Right."

"Then why do I only count 69 in this list here?" he asked as he gestured at the parchment.

"Idiot. Serah wasn't born until they got to Egypt."

They walked away still arguing with each other, but I decided not to follow them. I had heard other people had similar arguments before about when I was born. A lot of people seemed to think my mom was pregnant with me on the way to Egypt then gave birth to me once we arrived. I knew that to be false, but when I had tried to suggest to others having variations of this same conversation, no one would take me seriously when I suggested that maybe my uncles and cousins weren't always accurate in their records.

Anyway, I had my own work to do, and I needed to get to the market before all of the good figs were gone. The whole rest of the day, I kept shaking my head and laughing. Maybe I should have introduced myself to those foolish boys and told them the real story. My cousin was great at knowing how to make his letters and how to write our names. But I would never go to him for help with anything involving numbers! I'm not even sure if he could count his fingers and toes. And as far as singular and plural went, you pretty much had to go by context and not pay too much attention to which ending he used. One daughter, two daughters, what mattered to him was the concept of the relationship.

Sometimes I wonder if those two boys ever stopped to think about the fact that I couldn't have played the harp for my grandfather if I was still in my mother's womb. Maybe I could have sung. I don't know. I've never heard a baby in the womb sing, but that doesn't mean it couldn't happen. Who knows. All I know is I was definitely not an unborn baby on the way to Egypt. I remember all of the sand and the feelings of joy and anticipation even as we walked by people who were clearly hungry and miserable.

"Maybe," Osnat mused, "those boys were more like me than you. I love the stories and the laws in the Torah. I love the answers I can find in the Torah's words. But, every time I discover an answer, I find seven new questions have risen to my mind."

It's possible. I didn't want to contradict Osnat or get into even a mild verbal sparring with her. I needed Osnat to take my treasure, protect it, and keep the thread growing. I couldn't let something like this derail me now after waiting so long and coming so far.

Chapter 6 – Egypt

"Strangers in a Strange Land"

Pulled by the bond of blood
To another land of sand
Where it takes months
For me to understand
What our neighbors are saying,
The world flips upside down
As the son protects the father
And I
Still slip between others' legs
Weaving songs of love and strength.

Even though Joseph was a busy, powerful man in Egypt, he came out to personally greet us and escort us to our new home in the Goshen region of Egypt. My father and uncles had already had their chance for emotional hugs, and we all followed their lead and made a clear path for Jacob. I saw his walking stick start to wobble and could sense the trembling of his feet with each step forward. Then, suddenly, Joseph flung himself at the old man just as Jacob opened his arms wide.

"Is it really truly you, my son?" asked my grandfather as he tried to see past the beard and Egyptian clothing to the man underneath.

"Yes, father" replied the man dressed in finer clothes than I had ever seen before.

"You have your mother's eyes" I heard my grandfather whisper as the two walked away, wrapped in their own fragile, emotional reunion.

For the first few days, there seemed to be a sort of frantic pace to life. It was as if everyone felt they had to make up for years and years of separation as fast as possible. There was a stream of family gatherings where the adults would cluster around Joseph and shout over each other trying to tell him everything that had happened with them, their friends, and their families since he had disappeared. If they weren't pelting Joseph with information about their lives, they were tying him up with questions about what happened to him in all those years that he had been missing from our family.

With the adults busy crowding around Joseph, my brothers, cousins, and I ran off to play with Joseph's sons, Ephriam and Menashe. Ephraim and Menashe showed us all the places to hide, and as we peered out at the Egyptians around us, they explained what we were seeing. It was from Menashe and Ephraim that we learned to tell who the powerful people were, and who we should avoid running into. They taught us about Egyptian fashions, customs, and games. I would have gotten into all sorts of sticky situations if it weren't for my cousins. No one had to tell me not to sing when we went on these adventures, but I admit there were times when I couldn't help humming under my breath.

This time of increased freedom for me came to a gradual stop as Joseph returned to his duties rationing out the stored grain and other food. Some of my brothers and cousins got to join Menashe and Ephraim and their friends at lessons in other parts of town. But I was pulled back into the world of my mother, aunts, and grandmother. My grandmother and I resumed our private sessions together, and I came to understand my special gift a little bit better. (And yes, I confessed to Osnat, I did use my magic to help Joseph with the food rationing, especially as we reached the middle of the seventh year of the famine.)

One day, many years after we buried my beloved grandmother and my grandfather Jacob, my uncle Joseph gathered together my father and all of his brothers. I don't think Joseph had ever called all of his brothers together like this before. I could tell something big was happening. Like my great, great grandmother Sarah and so many other women, I strove to satisfy my curiosity by coming as close to the tent as I dared.

Pretending to doze off while leaning against the tent support with my ear pressed close, I eventually heard Joseph say, "I am about to die." Then, even after spending most of his life in Egypt, Joseph talked about how there would come a time when we would have to leave here. We were only here as visitors. And it was possible that we had only been treated as well as we had because of Pharoah's gratitude and affection for Joseph. With Joseph dying, we were about to lose our greatest protector in Egypt. Besides, our land was someplace else. Someplace that God had long ago promised to my grandfather Jacob, and his father and grandfather before him. Joseph was absolutely positive God would surely take notice of my family and bring us from Egypt to the land He promised on oath to my grandfathers. Then, Joseph made my uncles promise him that when they left Egypt, they would take his bones with them. I heard each of my uncles in turn promise

Joseph they would take his bones with them when they left. But my father and my uncles never left Egypt.

When we first came to Egypt, we all figured it would be just a temporary move. It would be a good way to reunite with Joseph and be close to the only source of food for miles around. But once we got there, our days fell into regular routines. Even once the famine was over in Egypt, at first we couldn't be sure it was over back in Canaan as well. And by the time we knew the famine had truly passed, our flocks were well established in Egypt and we had set down some roots and made some friends. Plus, the longer we stayed, the larger our family got. And as my brothers and my cousins got married, we gained not just babies but whole families of in-laws as well.

When Joseph died, there were members of the family who suggested it would be a good time to leave. But the Pharaoh was so grateful for all Joseph had done for him that our family enjoyed the privilege of royal favor for many years. When that Pharaoh was laid to rest in his burial chamber, his son ascended to power. The boy didn't really know why my family had been favored by his father, and it wasn't long before we were treated in the same manner as those around us, just another part of the greater Egyptian society.

Despite the passage of time, we never forgot who we were as a people. We remained loyal to God and maintained our family customs and stories. Many years after my uncle Joseph died, a new Pharaoh who did not know him came into power. Instead of being treated as honored distant relations to the royal court, we were soon treated worse than the poorest Egyptians we knew. This Pharaoh didn't use his wealth and power to help his people survive years of poor harvest or other hardships. All this Pharoah cared about was his own glory. He was desperate to be seen as so great and powerful that his legacy would be remembered throughout the generations. He started massive building projects, and when his advisors cautioned him about the cost of such endeavors, he started conscripting people to work for him and then stopped paying them.

Under the old Pharoah, my family had grown and thrived. Now we became a nation of slaves. My songs were not powerful enough to save those I loved. They only helped to make life just a little bit more bearable, a bit happier. I watched my brothers and my cousins weaken and die. As we buried them and were forced to return to work without the opportunity to properly mourn, I thought back to the day my grandfather looked me in the eyes, and said "My daughter, may death never prevail against you." Instead of a blessing, it felt like a curse.

As those around me aged and their bones began piling up under the sands of Egypt, I finally understood why my mother and grandmother had urged me to keep my gift a secret. Pharoah did not deal kindly with anyone who was the least bit powerful in any way unless that person was already under Pharoah's complete control. This king who called himself a God was already surrounded by magicians. It was clear that he liked to keep these magicians close to him even if most of them were just using tricks and not real magic. If Pharoah was using his magicians to help make life better for people, maybe I wouldn't have hidden from him so carefully. But Pharoah had his magicians curse those he viewed as enemies and inflict pain on those who incurred his displeasure.

My songs have always been intended to help others, not to hurt people. So, I learned to hide my gift as much as possible. Of course, I still did what I could to help people around me, but I kept my voice whisper-soft as I sang my incantations, and I stayed in the shadows as much as I could.

It's a good thing I hid my face as much as I could when any Egyptians were near, because even though I could have claimed to simply look like my mother and then my grandmother and even great-grandmother, someone would eventually get suspicious that they never saw the generations of my family together. Of course, there were always members of my extended family who knew who I was and how it was that I came to still be alive so many years after those born in the same year had long since ceased to walk this earth. They sent their children to sit at my feet and learn the stories of our family and our faith.

Then, during my people's darkest days, I discovered I was once again needed for more than just teaching the children about our people. There was a secret tradition passed down from my grandfather Jacob to Joseph, his favorite son. Tired of all the troubles that had befallen him as a result of this favoritism from his father, my uncle Joseph shared this secret tradition with his brothers rather than keeping it only for himself and for his own children.

While he was still alive, my father Asher passed this secret on to me. I had always assumed that he had also shared it with my brothers and that my uncles had shared it with their children. To this day, I'm not sure whether they did or not. All I know is that over time, I was the only one who remembered the words clearly.

When he pulled me aside to share this secret with me, my father told me that false leaders might try to trick us into following them and abandoning the beliefs of our ancestors. Only a true leader and redeemer of our people would come and say, "I surely remembered you." To keep this message safe, I turned these words and their significance into a song that I would sing to calm people down and heal aching hearts as everyone's spirits began to flag under the harsh decrees of Pharaoh. As I sang, I wrapped the words in veils of secrecy. When I fell silent after singing this song, people felt a glimmer of hope for the future and a belief that a redeemer would come to relieve us of our suffering. They knew I would be able to separate the true redeemer from pretenders; they knew I held the key to this knowledge in my song.

One day, some of the children came running over to me and tugged on my skirts. Jumping up and down, they told me there were rumors of strange things at the palace. They asked me if the redeemer had finally come to free us from Pharoah's cruelty. I couldn't answer them right away, but that evening after we finished our meal but before we all retreated to our own beds for the night, the elders came to find me.

"Serah," one elder said, "a certain man has come, and he has performed signs in our sight." They spoke of walking sticks that became snakes and then reverted to being sticks once more. They told me about the Nile river turning to blood, and other wonders they witnessed at the palace. I was fascinated by what they had witnessed, but I had to tell them that there is no reality in the signs. Just because this man and his brother had been granted an audience with Pharoah and had pleaded with him to let our people go, none of this indicated that the true redeemer had come at last.

Clearly, they were dismayed to hear my response, and they started to sadly slouch away. Then one of the elders stopped and turned back around.

"We have forgotten to tell her of the other unusual thing this man said," he reminded the others. A few scratched their heads. I had noticed their memory was not as sharp as it once had been. A few of the elders' eyes lit up. That's when they mentioned that this man, called Moses, had spoken not just to Pharoah, but also to them, the elders who were there. To them, he had said, "I surely remembered you."

My face lit up as I sang my song, not at a whisper this time, but loudly and clearly enough for everyone to hear the words. That was enough for them all to believe in God and in Moses as God's messenger and the redeemer of the Israelites.

Knowing the redeemer God had sent to bring us out of the slavery of Egypt was finally here lifted everyone's spirits at first. But, as Pharaoh thwarted Moses' attempts to lead us to freedom time and time again, we all began to feel a bit deflated. As the Egyptians were plagued with one type of disaster after another, we were still forced to lug bricks about, building these crazy structures to inflate and appease Pharoah's ego. Then, while the Egyptian houses were hidden in darkness so thick you could reach out and touch it, I noticed

Moses wandering around the city. For three days and three nights, Moses walked around the city, pausing here and there to squint at something or to stare intently at the ground.

On the third night, Moses bumped into me while staring at the ground. He almost knocked me over! But, when he looked up to apologize, I could see the exhaustion all over his face. Inviting him to sit down next to me for a moment, I asked him why he was so tired. He said "for 3 days and 3 nights I have been going around the city to find Joseph's coffin, and I haven't found it. We can't leave Egypt without it." As Moses spoke, I remembered my uncle Joseph making us swear this promise before he died.

Taking Moses' hand in mine, I said "come with me and I will show you where it is." I led him to the river and told him that the Egyptian wizards threw it in the river here when the current Pharaoh had come to power. I think he knew without me saying it that I had hidden on the banks of the river, watching from between the reeds as the Egyptian wizards sought to curry Pharaoh's favor, saying to Pharoah "it's your wish that the nation of Israelites won't ever leave here but will stay to do the heavy labor and to follow your every command. We have heard that if they don't find the bones of Joseph, they will never be able to leave." And with those words, they flung Joseph's marble coffin into the depths of the Nile River.

I pointed to the exact spot where the Egyptian magicians had stood, and Moses immediately stood on the bank of the river in the exact same spot. He called out

"Joseph! Joseph! You know how you made Israel swear *'When God has taken notice of you, you shall carry up my bones from here.'* Honor the God of Israel and don't prevent the redemption of the Israelites! You have the credit of good deeds, ask mercy from your Creator and come up from the depths!"

Immediately, Joseph's coffin began to bubble up and rise from the depths like a reed. Moses took it and put it on his shoulder and as soon as Pharoah relented and said we could leave, all of Israel followed Moses and Joseph's coffin out of Egypt, just as we had followed Joseph into Egypt all those hundreds of years before.

Chapter 7 – Exodus

"On your mark, get set..."

Muscles awake
Shaking off
Centuries-old cramps
And the heart
Pumps in time
To the hurried whispers
"It's time!"
To claim our birthright.

With all of the many wonders I had already seen in my life, you might think by the time we finally left Egypt, I would have become jaded to God's miracles. But that was not the case. I had seen the effects my songs could have on others. I saw people who were at death's door get out of bed and perform difficult physical feats. I had witnessed the power of childbirth and the resilience of people against all odds. I had seen rainbows and wonders of light in the sky above me. Plus, like everyone else alive in Egypt, at that time, I had experienced the strange series of plagues and marveled at the mighty power of God.

I heard some people say they thought the Nile River turning to blood was the craziest thing they had ever seen in their lives, even though Pharaoh's magicians had been able to mimic God's power to turn the water red. Each of the other plagues also had their champions. Then there were those who thought being guided by pillars of fire and smoke was the most miraculous thing that had ever occurred since the creation of the world. All of these things were indeed incredible, and it's hard for me to describe to you the feeling of power that crackled in the air during those days. But, for me, they paled in comparison to what came next.

There are a lot of different stories that circulated about exactly what happened. We all agreed, God was the true power behind what happened. But as for which of us served as God's conduit, I suppose you'll have to make up your own mind. Between all of us, there was probably enough adrenaline around to raise the level of the Dead Sea by a whole cubit.

News that Pharaoh had finally relented and was letting us go spread through the whole camp faster than any fire I have ever seen. Things were a blur as everyone rushed to grab as much as they could carry.

At first, there was a sense of elation among the crowd. But then, someone with keen hearing said he heard something behind us. So some of the children turned to look. That's when the shouting and panic began. Pharaoh was racing after us in a chariot. We could see the light glinting off of swords in between the puffs of sand being thrown off by the horses hooves. We were running as fast as we could when suddenly the people in the front skidded to a stop. There was a huge sea blocking our way. As you might imagine, panic set in pretty quickly.

Maybe that's why no one knows exactly what happened. Moses raised his staff and spread open his arms at the same time that I was putting all of my strength into my singing and a man named Nachshon just kept on running into the water. Then, suddenly, Nachshon wasn't neck-deep in the water anymore. The water moved itself into two large walls towering above our heads, and at our feet appeared a path free of water.

My pace slowed as I walked on that path. I don't know how I kept my song going as my mouth hung open in wonderment. There were fish of every size, shape, and color making the water look like a rippling rainbow. But the walls of water held fast, and not even a drop touched my head or my calves. It didn't even seem odd to me when I noticed that the round belly of the woman walking next to me had become completely transparent, and a baby not yet ready to be born gazed at the fish with eyes just as wide as mine.

I don't usually like to correct the sages that rose up as leaders of our community centuries after that moment I spent between the walls of water alive with God's marvelous creations. But I just couldn't help myself the time I heard Rabbi Yochanan teaching his students about the miracle we experienced at the sea. Somehow, he had gotten it in his head that when the waters of the Red Sea formed walls on our left and right, the only way they could possibly have stood up straight like that was if they resembled a window lattice or an impervious net.

There is no way that witnessing this miracle through some type of lattice or net could have been even half as powerful as what really happened. So, I stepped forward and let both Rabbi Yochanan and all of his students know that I was there, and the water was not as a net, but as transparent windows. After I did my best to paint them a picture of that day with words (and maybe a bit of magical humming to help), I slipped back into the crowd and went to do the rest of my errands, satisfied that now there would be at least one person who could carry on that particular memory after I am gone.

Looking at the woman in front of me, I added "I probably don't need to say this Osnat, but I think you will do a far better job as custodian of these memories than those men are doing."

She smiled and we continued calmly and quietly on our journey.

Chapter 8 - Inheritance in Israel

"Coming Home"

This sand between my weary toes
Feels different
Than the years of sand
Encrusted in my wrinkles
And clogging my lungs.
These grains
no different than their neighbors
In other eyes
Embed themselves
In my heart,
My own small piece
Of promised land.

A dove gently landed on Osnat's shoulder and rubbed its beak along her chin. I was mesmerized by this simple expression of familiarity and affection. I don't even think Osnat realized the way the corners of her mouth pulled slightly up toward her shining eyes. I realized I was being granted a rare glimpse of Osnat at peace, with her guard down. If I hadn't already made up my mind she was the right person to entrust with my memories and my legacy, that particular moment would have been enough to do so.

With the dove still resting its beak against her cheek, Osnat turned her head slightly, and we both realized the light outside was fading. Reaching into a small, plain box on her desk, Osnat took out what looked like a spray of millet and offered it to the dove. When the dove took the treat in its mouth, I could have sworn it bobbed its head in thanks before taking its leave.

I gratefully accepted Osnat's offer of dinner and a comfortable place to sleep. When I was younger, I might have stayed awake all night not just talking, but singing and dancing as well. But, while my grandfather blessed me with long life, he did not bless me with eternal youth. You may think this a rather unfortunate lack of foresight but the truth is, I appreciated the fact I now looked like an old woman and had looked old for hundreds of years now. A woman covered in wrinkles has a lot more freedom than a rosy-cheeked maiden to come and go and do things which may seem eccentric to others. And while I knew, based on past experiences, that neither skipping a meal nor sleeping in less than ideal conditions would bring the angel of death to finally take me, when given the chance, I would always opt to accept such gracious hospitality.

Over dinner, our conversation was more generic and more personal than it had been in Osnat's office. It was almost as if we were getting to know each other in a way that ran opposite to most people. I had already shared some of my most intimate secrets with the woman sharing her bread and vegetables with me. But we knew next to nothing about one another's loves or children, topics with which so many women begin their friendships.

Osnat laughed with understanding when I told her none of those men who thought themselves the keepers of our people's history could agree on the simple question of whether I married or had children. The scribes had kept such careful records for my brothers and my male cousins that hundreds and even thousands of years later, both the numbers of their descendants and even some of their names were known to people who never met them. My brothers each had large families, like my grandfather, and they had fifty-three thousand and four hundred descendants before people stopped counting.

After a good night's sleep, Osnat and I returned to her office in the yeshiva to continue our conversation. When we got there, Osnat pulled out a large scroll of parchment. Her eyes flew over the letters, which danced before her. With a bow, the letters settled back onto the parchment, and after a short pause, Osnat raised her eyes to mine. "You are mentioned here, though," she gestured to the scroll. "Your name is listed in the genealogy. Such a rare honor that one might have thought our people consisted of only men back then." I smiled and admitted that was, indeed, true. I might have wished my descendants were named as a clan and counted just like my brothers, but my name will not be forgotten. So ridiculous the way men refused to even consider calling my brood "the family of the Serahites." But I suppose Osnat was right in pointing out that she could plainly see my large family was, indeed alluded to in the scroll through my inclusion on the list of Asher's descendants.

"You know," said Osnat, "your name has preceded you. While I had no idea what you looked like, or if you were still alive, and hadn't heard any of the stories that you have shared with me, I had heard your name before. My father used to mention you as an example of someone who is charitable and makes a positive difference in the world. And now that we've met, I know he was right."

I didn't know how to respond to that. I wasn't used to hearing praises from people I'd never met. When I was still a child, I was accustomed to being thanked if I made someone feel better. But, since leaving Egypt, people seemed to have mostly forgotten about me. Or so I had thought. As the silence started to stretch into being awkward, I felt it was time for me to continue my story.

To my mind, there's not much to say about the years we spent wandering in the desert. At first, the strange manna we ate each day was a wondrous novelty. But, over time, it, grew just as monotonous as the sand dunes and the miraculous pillars of smoke and fire that accompanied us.

When we finally reached the land of Israel, I was surprised to learn the fact that Asher was my adoptive father, and not my biological one turned to my advantage. While it had never been a secret my mother had me with her first husband before he died and she married Asher, I had always thought of myself solely as Asher's daughter. He was a good father to me. His family was my family. I never really thought about the fact my brothers were only half-brothers and not my full brothers. But, if I had been the daughter of Asher himself, I would not have inherited a portion in the Land of Israel. Only my brothers would have been able to lay claim to the land.

To this day, even though I was forced to leave it much later during the wars, I hold my small piece of the Land in Israel close to my heart as one of my most precious possessions.

Osnat smiled in recognition of the feeling. In her case, though, it was not land that gave her that feeling but her studies of the sacred texts. She told me she had even figured out how to limit her childbearing to only two children so she could devote herself to her studies. I told her I thought that showed even more wisdom than others attributed to me.

For years there were women who came to me to learn from my wisdom. And, not to brag, but it was my wisdom that helped our people more than the weapons in their hands when we waged war with Joab. What happened was I called from the edge of the city, and told all who were listening to Joab to come to me so I could speak to him. As I expected, he came just like I had asked. Once I knew it was really him, I told him he should stop this foolish fighting. Clearly he hadn't learned that our people believe when you come close to a city prepared to fight against it, you are first supposed to proclaim peace and see if you can sort things out that way.

At first Joab didn't want to listen to me or take what I said seriously. But this was one of the increasingly rare times when I decided to tell him who I really was. Not the full story, not nearly as much as I told Osnat, but I did tell him "I am the one full of the faith of Israel. I am the one who completed the number of Israelites in Egypt. I am the one who was trusted by Joseph and Moses. And you want to kill a city and a mother in Israel...." He didn't want to lose face in front of his men, but he did listen to me in the end.

I confided in Osnat that I no longer had the energy I once had to hold all of these memories on my own. A long life does not have to mean an eternal life. I have heard the whispers of another who death did not prevail upon but who no longer walks this plane of existence either. It's time for me to move on to a new phase of my life now, whatever that might look like.

After a cup of tea and assurances from Osnat that my legacy was safe with her, I took my leave from her with a smile in my eyes and a lightness in my heart.

Chapter 9 – Legacy

"Epilogue"

We rarely know
How our own stories end
Or what threads
Get woven into future generations.
We can only hope
The memory of our songs
And the stories we shared
Continue to live.

Soon after Serah left Osnat's side, a fiery chariot approached her as she made her way along the road. A hand reached out to her, and when their fingers clasped, she felt herself being gently helped into the magnificent chariot. Thus Jacob's blessing came true as Serah was not buried in the ground but whisked to a heavenly palace.

In this palace, it is said that all of the righteous of Israel live. Serah bat Asher has her own set of chambers, where she is surrounded by many thousands and thousands of women who merit to be with her.

Three times a day, the announcement comes: The likeness of Josef the tzadik is coming! With joy she goes out, to that curtained area which is dedicated to her, and observes light that looks like her uncle Joseph. With joy she greets it, saying, "Happy was that day, when I gave the tidings before my grandfather that you were still alive!"

Then she returns to the rest of the women, and they all sing the praises of God. They talk with one another about how many places and joys each and every one of them had! Then they turn their attention to studying the sacred texts of their people.

Maybe someday, Serah thinks, she'll make another visit to the mortal realm.

Endnote:
Source Materials Consulted

While some aspects of this book come from my own imagination, many of the events and stories incorporated into this volume originate in biblical and rabbinic sources. To explore these for yourself, see:

On Serah's place in the family and that she both went down and came out of Egypt:

Genesis 46:6-7 and 46:17 and related commentaries
Tur HaAroch Genesis 46:7:1 and 46:17:1
Rashi on Genesis 46:7:1
Ramban on Genesis 46:7:1
Rabeinu Bahya, Shemot 18:6:1
Or Hahayim on Genesis 46:7:3
Or Hahayim on Genesis 46:7:4
Daat Zekanim on Genesis 46:7:1

Numbers 26:44-47 and related commentaries
Chizkuni Numbers 26:46:1
Rashi on Numbers 26:46:1
Ramban on Numbers 26:46:1
Midrash Aggadah Numbers 26:46:1
Daat Zekanim on Numbers 26:46:1
Seder Olam Rabbah 9:2

Regarding Serah and Jacob:

Genesis 45:25-27
Sefer HaYashar, book of Genesis, Vayigash
Targum Jonathan Numbers 26:46
Zohar 3:167b:5

Serah's Knowledge in Egypt:

Shemot Rabbah 5:13
Genesis 50:24-25
Devarim Rabbah 11:7

Serah and crossing the sea:

Pesikta d'Rav Kahana 11:13

Other mentions of Serah:

2 Samuel 20:15-22
Rashi on 2 Samuel 20:19:1
Kohelet Rabbah 9:18:2
Kav Hayashar 15:3, 54:9 - 12

Osnat's full name is Osnat Barzani. Information about her can be found both online
(e.g. https://en.wikipedia.org/wiki/Asenath_Barzani) and in the recently published (Levine Querido; Illustrated edition, 2021) "Osnat and Her Dove: The True Story of the World's First Female Rabbi" by Sigal Samuel (Author) and Vali Mintzi (Illustrator)

Author Profile

Already an accomplished poet, and author of five published volumes of poetry, this is Rabbi Suzanne Brody's fictional narrative debut.

She draws her inspiration from deep within the Jewish tradition, and her work is also influenced by her undergraduate years at Wellesley College, her PhD studies in neuroscience at UCSD, and her rabbinical training at the Ziegler School of Rabbinic Studies.

www.ingramcontent.com/pod-product-compliance
Lightning Source LLC
Chambersburg PA
CBHW050209130526
44590CB00043B/3349